Coláiste Oideachais Mhuire Gan Smal

Luimneach

prayer from where we are

WITNESS BOOK 13

Christian Experience Series

PRAYER FROM WHERE WE ARE

SUGGESTIONS ABOUT THE POSSIBILITY AND PRACTICE OF PRAYER TODAY

by JAMES CARROLL

1970.

PFLAUM / STANDARD
38 West Fifth Street, Dayton, Ohio 45402

Cover Photo: International News Photo.
Paul Tucker: pp. 14, 19, 25, 29, 30, 39, 44,
49, 57, 58, 63, 69, 73, 74, 87, 88, 94, 118
Wide World Photos: 7, 81, 103
UPI Photos: frontispiece, pp. 93, 111

Design by David Sweeney

Nihil Obstat: Rev. Joseph B. Collins, S. S., S. T. D.
            Censor Deputatus

Imprimatur: Patrick Cardinal O'Boyle
            Archbishop of Washington
            1970

Library of Congress Catalog Card Number: 71-133402

© 1970 by National Office of Confraternity of Christian Doctrine,
Washington, D. C.

ISBN 0-8278-2120-4
12120/25M/S10M-2-473

TABLE OF CONTENTS

1 THE SEARCH FOR PRAYER TODAY   1

2 THE PROBLEM IS NOT PRAYER   15

3 TENDING THE PRESENCE OF GOD   31

4 FAITHFULNESS AND SPONTANEITY   45

5 THE TENDING SILENCE   59

6 THE TENDING SOLITUDE, THE TENDING GROUP   75

7 THE TENDING IMAGINATION   89

8 SUMMARY: THE PRACTICE OF PRAYER TODAY   105

   SUGGESTIONS FOR FURTHER READING   119

CHAPTER ONE

the search for prayer today

"It's a new world, and only what was true of the old one will survive." Or so I was told recently by one of the young people I serve at a huge urban university. Whether the new world represents the birth of truth or yet another death of it is not the question. Our question is simpler: Can the human activity we call *prayer* survive in the new world? The purpose of this booklet is to explore the possibility, not only that prayer can survive, but that the new world is crying out for a true and sensible experience of prayer.

The discovery that all share these days is powerful and undeniable. It is the discovery that we are strangers in a strange place. We may not know what this means, but we feel down to our toes that something very new has taken hold of us. It is not just that important new things have come upon us so rapidly—that men have actually walked on the moon, for instance—but that important old ones have gone. All kinds of certainties and tested values have abandoned us like faithless friends——or we have abandoned them. Many of us feel as Columbus must have felt; exhilarated to have our feet planted on brand new soil, but anxious to get safely home again.

But home for us is not something we can *return* to. Even the sixties, tumultuous though they were, are part of the good old days now. Home is ahead of us, not back. The pace and the quality of the upheaval we live with are signs that the most profoundly human values are waiting to be seized and cherished. Not least of these, and, perhaps——who knows?——the greatest, is the value we call *prayer*.

Rollo May writes, "When an age is torn loose from its moorings and more and more people are thrown back upon themselves, more and more people can take steps to find and realize themselves."[1] From almost every perspective, and certainly from the perspective of life in the Spirit, our age has indeed been torn loose from its moorings. Not so long ago, just a fad or two back, intelligent men began telling

[1]Rollo May, *Love and Will* (New York: Norton, 1969), p. 17.

us that our very roots in the transcendent had been cut off, and that the very idea of *prayer* was outmoded. The churches, whose main function in society has been to institutionalize respect for the spirit-life and to nurture the life of prayer, are either collapsing or so worried about collapsing that they have no time for anything else. So, when it comes to the question of prayer, individual men and women indeed have been thrown back upon themselves.

For centuries our church and our culture have schooled us in the "proper" ways to approach the transcendent. It is very startling, then, suddenly to find that the very idea of the transcendent is up for grabs. Because this is so startling, because it has thrown so many people at least slightly off-balance, we should not be surprised that the search for prayer today takes extreme forms. Young people take flight from the past, often using the future and their youth as hiding places. Older people seek refuge, often with some rigidity, in a past their children never knew, a past which included real, if rather commonplace, contemplation. Perhaps we could all regain our balance if we realized that the widow who hoards St. Ann's oil and never misses Wednesday's seven-thirty novena is exploring the same uncharted territory that a nineteen-year-old student is trying to find through experiments with drugs. They both are looking for a way to pray.

The preoccupation with the transcendent that characterizes many these days, especially the young, is remarkable. But even more remarkable, I believe, is the *lack* of such preoccupation now characterizing the churches. Many of those long regarded within the churches as "people of prayer"—ministers, priests, sisters, and religious of all kinds—acknowledge casually that, while prayer forms part of their history, it is no longer a real part of their present. Thus, as more and more individuals find themselves grappling with the prayer-question, the obvious representatives of the great religious traditions seem increasingly unprepared to help them. Writing about prayer, for instance, while it has continued, has continued mainly in the vein of another time. Of the important subjects for which the churches claim stewardship, only the subject of prayer has not experienced the upheaval of a serious effort at rethinking. The attention of the churches has been taken up with other things. Unfortunately the churches presumed that their age-old corner on the prayer-market would continue. It has not. One prominent Christian, disturbed by what he considered the lack of prayer among church-persons, was moved to ask, "Do only atheists and young persons know the silence of contemplation?"[2] I believe that atheists and young persons and believers and old persons and even some church-persons know that silence. And many more are looking for it.

People today are seeking, as people always have, a way of knowing and caring and living that is extrahuman. But many of them have given up looking in customary forms of Christian devotion. The most visible quest for the extrahuman is occurring within the counterculture of youth. If older people could stop their loud and frenzied preoccupation with the

[2]Michael Novak, "Where Did All The Spirit Go?" in Commonweal, vol. 40, no. 20 (Sept. 5, 1969), p. 542.

antics of the young and really look at this counter-culture, they might discover that some of the cherished values of our tradition are alive within it and waiting to be nourished. One of these is prayer.

Many of the phenomena associated with the freak-culture can be understood as marks of the spirit's search for the Spirit. Young people are certainly not building a new religion, nor are they enamored of the old religion in any form. But their struggle for sense in a senseless world inevitably faces them with what can be recognized as classic religious yearnings. Andrew Greeley, Michael Novak, Peter Berger, and others have shown how the drug-rock-hip culture repeats the patterns of a human quest for mystical union with God.

The aspect of the youth-culture that older Americans find most disturbing is the intensely political righteousness with which students approach life. In the late sixties, student political protests occurred with such regularity that Walter Cronkite of C.B.S. news began to say each night, "Today's campus

disruption took place at . . . ." What is of crucial importance about the political campus today is that it is not merely political at all. As Michael Novak has intuited,[3] the new politics of the university is new because it is shot through with a new mysticism. Politics is essentially the process of making human life human. Implicit in the radical politics of the college headliner is what I believe to be a remarkable awareness that human life, to be human, must attend to the extrahuman. The whole point of a dean's office seizure is missed unless one takes into account the sacred-psychedelic paraphernalia that accompany it.

It is my experience that many of the very people who are setting the political style of universities are simultaneously and in the same movement the people who are, as one of them put it to me, "into God." Drugs, astrology, numerology, rock music, yoga, zen diet, I-ching are now the marks of identity for the young adults who in another time would have led food-riots and panty-raids. These days they wear

[3]Michael Novak, *A Theology of Radical Politics* (New York: Herder and Herder, 1969), pp. 122-128.

red armbands, they sit-in, they use foul language, and, apparently, they try to pray.

What remains undecided is the response that these young people are going to get from the adherents of the old world culture that produced them and against which they are reacting. In the early seventies two unfortunate responses seem to have the edge. The first response to the freak in our midst is outright, blatant hatred. This is typified in the film, *Easy Rider,* in which the all-American bigot murders two young long-hairs. The second response is at once more subtle and more cynical. It is the response of Peter Max and Boston's Freaque-Boutique and the whole army of buyers and sellers who recognize in the youth revolution only a new and profitable market-place. Rebellion becomes a sales pitch. Youth's most dangerous adversary is not the red-necked bigot but the side-burned barker.

A truly human response to the counterculture of youth would be both nourishing and critical. Such a response should come above all from the community of faith who can recognize a quest of the spirit as its own. One who has accepted the struggle of prayer as his own struggle already knows what the struggle of young people is about.

Ironically it is the elderly people in our culture who are in the best position—or so it seems to me—to understand and accept the strange searchings of youth. The elderly, as we still find them in the Catholic tradition at any rate, are characterized by a faithful clinging to religious forms of the past. Their quest for prayer takes the form more often of novenas than numerology. Yet in their own way, they are as misunderstood and as attacked as are young people. These are people who know better when zealous young priests rant that candles are superstition and that the rosary is magic, for they have known real prayer with the fire and the beads. These are people who only smiled when most of us wondered, half in mourning, if God were really dead. Hidden in lonely one-room flats or in the far wing of some rest home, or on the winterized porch of in-laws, these people are not loud or colorful in their search for the transcendent. They are the unnoticed contemplatives of our time.

Confusion about prayer, and frustration in the search for it is most deep-seated and widespread among the middle people of our culture. They have neither the gusto of late adolescence nor the inner stillness of old age as aids to seeking the transcendent. In addition the middle people carry the burden of the details that consume our days. They are the worriers and the workers, the ones who pay most dearly for the changes besetting us. Michael Novak writes, "One senses the absence of the life of prayer everywhere in middle-aged groups: married persons, priests, activists of all sorts."[4] These are the people who will tell you simply that they do not pray anymore and that they do not miss it a bit. Yet there prevails a sense, for me at least, that these are the people who, if only out of the corners of their eyes, are watching closely the new outbreak of yearning after transcendence. They have known prayer and

[4]Novak, "Where Did All The Spirit Go?" p. 540.

they miss it. The search for prayer today is pursued most intensely by the young, most quietly by the old. But it involves us all. It is everyone's search.

QUESTIONS FOR DISCUSSION

1. Do you think that many Catholics today are concerned about their prayer? Are they too shy to admit it (it is never mentioned as one of the topics people want discussed in sermons, lectures, etc.)? Do you feel uncomfortable talking about prayer? If so, how would you account for it?

2. Have your habits and/or style of prayer changed in the last few years? If so, how? Do you feel it is a change for the better?

3. In the last few years, many churches have done away with vigil lights, candles, and devotions such as public novenas. Do you think this has been good or not? Has it caused people to pray less? Do you think that the changes in the liturgy have been helpful or harmful to praying? Why?

4. Have you ever stopped praying for a long period

of time? Why or why not? If you did, how do you feel about it now?

5. Have you ever consulted anyone about praying? If so, was it helpful? How?

6. Do you think that using drugs could be a valid aid in the search for a true experience of prayer? Why or why not?

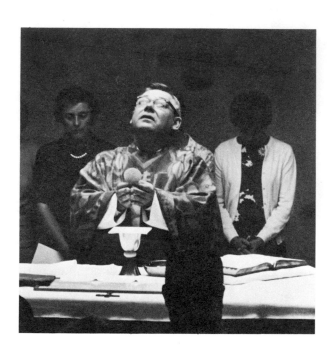

CHAPTER TWO

the problem is not prayer

The risk in trying to solve the problem of prayer in our time is that one might seem to succeed. One might actually uncover a solution or two. I have, for example, thought at various times that my own frustration in praying might be eased by a new set of formulas or a better technique. Once I went on a diet, not to lose weight but to learn to pray. All I learned, finally, was hunger, and all I succeeded in doing was transplanting God from heaven to my stomach.

Some have suggested that our confusion about prayer would be solved if only we altered our prayer vocabulary. The old language, with its simple and naive images like "father" and "heaven," has been rejected here and there in favor of a language of vague and hard-to-imagine abstractions. In the end this erudite response to the problem of prayer amounts only to substituting a theology of prepositions for a theology of nouns. To discover that all the talk about God "in" or "beyond" does not improve much on the classic line that prayer is "lifting one's mind and heart to God," is to discover that the problem is not primarily one of language.

The fact is that our problem is not with prayer at all. Our problem is that we have accepted as normal what Rollo May calls a "schizoid world." The schizoid world is the world in which the continuity between the polarities of our existence—between person and community, body and spirit—has been broken and lost. We have come to be controlled by our tendency to treat such polarities as oppositions, to break up what is in fact a natural unity.

This dichotomizing tendency wreaks havoc in all areas of human life, including prayer. For example, hot arguments have been going on for centuries about the value of community prayer versus private prayer because we have lost hold of the continuity between our inner selves and each other, between the life of the private individual and the life of the group. When private prayer and community prayer are seen as rivals, one or other seems to seek exclusive sway. When that happens, as it has today with private prayer being the loser, the precious balance of complementaries which are absolutely essential to each other is lost. Undoubtedly one of the major reasons why the liturgical reform of the sixties proved so disappointing was that it was pursued with no regard for the reform of the practice of private prayer. The two need each other.

The same dichotomizing tendency has stifled the growth of prayer in other ways, too. There is apparent conflict between what we used to call "mental prayer" and "vocal prayer" because we have lost hold of the continuity between the silence and the word. There is apparent conflict between "prayers of petition" and "prayers of praise" because we have lost hold of the continuity between simple human receiving and simple human giving. Prayer-talk shares in the continuing confusion of our man-talk and our God-talk.

But the most destructive dichotomy, the one with the farthest reaching effects on the religious life of our world, is the one which opposes service and prayer. This is in a way quite different from the opposition set up in the past between "contemplation" and "action." More and more these days, people describe their prayer as "the work I do" or "life itself" or the like. Certainly the Christian tradition can amply support the statement that "to work is to pray," but to say that prayer is *only* serving others is to say, in the end, nothing about it. No doubt one of the magnificent graces of our time has been the rediscovery by Christians of their responsibility for the world. A church which does not see itself as a "serving church" distorts its gospel mission. Social and humanitarian action forms the most integral part of a man's loving response to God, for the response of love always implies real and concrete action. The mandate of Jesus extends to working for the welfare of the whole family of man, on which God pours his love without favoritism. But Jesus also spoke about

the cherished "secret place" where God is met alone.

For me the fact of prayer flows from the New Testament affirmation that God, the Father of Jesus, is present to us as love. The response of a "faith-full" man to that presence is attention. It does not matter how the presence of God is described, whether hierarchically ("above," "up there") or concentrically ("in," "within"). God is, as Bonhoeffer put it, present as the "beyond in our midst." When we pay attention to the "midst" (that is, to the neighbor, to the world), we are said to be serving. When we pay attention to the "beyond," we are praying. For the man of faith, the "beyond" and the "midst" are not in opposition; his responses of service and prayer are elements of the same movement. For the remainder of these pages, I will say little about attention to the needs of the neighbor, not because it is unimportant, but because my concern here is with the presence of the *beyond*. Today's Christian knows that without service there can be no true prayer.

What we seem to be forgetting is that without prayer there can be no *true* service.

The sentence just written, in addition to being an unfashionable one, is a difficult one. It seems to deny to the nonbelieving humanist the possibility of serving the neighbor truly. We know from experience that some of the most faithful servants of mankind, are secular humanists—people who do not explicitly recognize the presence of God or of any "beyond" in their midst. Nevertheless, I maintain that however noble and true the service of such humanists might be, it will always lack a crucial human dimension as long as it does not attend to the extrahuman. If this seems parochial or triumphal, I do not intend it to. If it seems to say that a New Testament faith claims to see more deeply into life than secular humanism, I accept that as so.

What faith claims to see is not additional data about life, not a set of special solutions to human problems. What faith claims to see is at once less and much more than that, for faith claims to see within and beyond human existence a person who is like a loving father. Indeed for faith, human existence has its final meaning as the gift, as the expression, as the revelation of that person.

Do you remember those puzzle pages that came in the comic section of the Sunday newspaper? Every once in a while they printed a game that consisted of a picture, say, of a family on a picnic. There would be trees and clouds and a picnic table and an automobile and Mom and Dad and Sue and John. Under this simple cartoon scene there would be a line that said, "Can you find the picture of the man hidden in this picnic-scene?" At first you would not see it. You would stare, and you would turn the page upside down and stare some more. But then, suddenly, an edge of the clouds became an ear and a branch of the tree a smiling mouth, and, by golly, from an angle there he was—a man. Once you saw that face, the simple picnic scene was never quite the same, for you had met the man. You had seen him.

Faith is something like that. For Christians there is a man hidden in every scene, and his name is Jesus. Once he has been met and seen, no scene, no "seeing," is quite the same again. Once Christ leaps alive, there is nothing human that is not the utterance of the divine. So delicate an utterance is it that the divine is never the denial of the human, but only the fulfillment of it. "Seeing Christ in others," as we used to say with no self-consciousness, is not seeing Christ at all unless it is simultaneously and truly seeing the other. Every experience of the "midst" becomes in this way a hint of the "beyond." The perennial temptation of Christians to affirm the beyond, to "see Christ," at the expense of the midst or by denial of the neighbor, is a temptation against real faith.

Faith is seeing more than is before the eyes. It thrives on what Peter Berger[1] calls the "signals of transcendence." Even the commonest experiences— laughter, childish hopes, fear, boredom—take on a new dimension. They are relished for themselves,

[1]Peter Berger, *A Rumor of Angels* (New York: Doubleday, 1969).

which means they are relished both as pointers within and pointers beyond.

The beyond, the transcendent to which the signs of human life point, is, for the Christian, neither a vague philosophical abstraction nor an impersonal, all-encompassing force. The transcendent whose signals we both are and seek is the Father of Jesus. He is the one to whom we can relate personally through service and prayer because we share in Jesus' relationship to him. Thus faith makes the discovery that all of human life takes on its true character when it is known and accepted and experienced as relatedness to the Father.

Michael Novak writes that "There is a difference between faith as a set of blinders and faith as a set of eye-openers."[2] We know that all too often *faith* is made to mean an unquestioning and submissive (not so much to God, but to hierarchs) approach to life. I would suggest that a test of faith, a way of discovering whether we wear blinders or eye-openers, is to look at what prayer is in our lives.

[2]Novak, "Where Did All The Spirit Go?" p. 540.

The kind of spirit-life we live will depend on the kind of faith-life we live. Prayer is an exact barometer of any man's Christian life.

Some people say, with implied apology, that they find themselves unable to pray. Such people usually think that they are confessing a failure of their own. That may be so, but it is also likely that they are reflecting on the kind of faith that has been nurtured in them by their time-and-place experience of the Church. Sadly many of us have had a blinding and inhibiting "faith," which has operated as a set of blinders, inflicted on us since childhood. It is no wonder prayer is often stillborn.

If faith is mainly a matter of meeting the man Jesus by plunging so fully into the midst that the beyond breaks in, prayer is a spontaneous reaction, primarily the reaction of listening, and "through listening," as Balthasar says, "learning how to answer."[3] If prayer, though, is a matter of making merits or making up for sins, or if prayer has absolutely no meaning in our lives, we come back to

[3]Hans Urs von Balthasar, *Prayer* (New York: Sheed & Ward, 1961), p. 12.

where we were a short time ago; the problem is not prayer. We wish it was, because at least there are techniques to be tried. The problem, though, is with the quality of our faith. For us that is another way of saying that the problem is with the quality of our humanness. But one of the nicest things about God is that he accepts us where we are. This means that even with dichotomizing, somewhat "schizoid," somewhat "self-blindered" people, prayer, true and sensible, is still possible.

QUESTIONS FOR DISCUSSION

1. Do you feel guilty when you have not prayed for a day or so? When you have not said any prayers? If so, why? Do you think you should feel guilty?
2. How would you define prayer?
3. A group of Catholics, all of whom had engaged in extra religious activities such as the Catholic Family Movement, cursillos, etc., all agreed that they had experienced God's presence in their lives *only* in a group experience of mutual caring.

Do you agree? Can we only find God in other people? Can we find God without trying to improve the quality of our relationships toward and service of other people?

4. Does a secular humanist who never prays live a less human life than a believer who prays regularly?

5. Do you think that your faith has operated in any way as a "set of blinders"? As a "set of eye-openers"?

6. Do you think that prayer is generally used as an excuse for inaction?

CHAPTER THREE

tending the presence of god

We take words for granted. We pull them out of our mind's back drawer and use them now and then and discard them. We rarely notice the words we use, and that is a shame because some words are wells of wisdom. Down through the years, some words have caught and held the creative insights of countless people. People have taken words and chiseled them and played with them and twisted them—all in an effort to catch for themselves and pass on to others something important.

For me one seemingly ordinary word is so rich and strong as to open up the whole discussion of prayer. It is a small word with huge implications. It is the word "tend." So many people have invested so much in "tend" that it comes to us with a galaxy of meanings and in a variety of forms· "attend," "retend," "attention," "retention," "tender," "intend," "intention," "intensity," "tension." By taking this jewel of a word and letting it catch light from several angles, we can, I think, learn again what prayer is all about.

Prayer is tending the presence of God. Prayer is tending *toward* the presence of God. Prayer is paying attention to the presence of God. Prayer is intending God's presence. Prayer is being tender with—being a tender of—God's presence. Prayer is living with the tension of God's presence. Prayer is living intensely with God's presence.

The verb "to tend" has both an active and a passive sense. In its active sense it means to take care of, to minister to, to cultivate. Men tend sheep and they tend flowers. The implication here is that a man assumes responsibility for something. When a man "tends" in this sense, he accepts a role of nurturing. What he nurtures is given into his hands. What he nurtures is helpless, submits to his care. It is what a nurse does when she "tends" her patients; it is what parents do when they "tend" their children;

and, I believe, it is what a man of faith does when he prays.

We are not accustomed to thinking of God as being helpless before men, yet there is a way in which he has made himself so. This is the helplessness, the submission, that is symbolized for Christians by the coming of Jesus in a feedbox and his departing on a pole. God's presence in the world is helpless before man. The fact of our freedom means that we can choose to ignore the beyond in our midst. We can refuse to tend it. Tending is not mere custodianship. It involves creativity; it is a matter of nurturing growth. The tending professions, whether flower-growing or medicine, imply gentle creativity. The manifestation of God, clothed in mystery as it always is, has been given over to man's tender care. We know that the coming kingdom will happen only in and through the cooperation of men. And so it is with the kingdom that is already present. God is met in prayer only when men tend his presence actively. God's presence must be sought out, rooted out, pursued as if it were a sheep in hiding, or a lost coin, or a hidden treasure. God is not plainly visible or neatly available to us. It is as if he waits us out in all the million dark corners of our existence. Finding God is hard, hard almost as growing orchids.

Another meaning of the active verb "to tend" is "to lean toward." The leaves of a massive tree all tend in harmony toward the source of light, life, and food—the sun. Tending in this sense is marked by gentleness, openness, desire. It is not so much an action as an attitude. The scriptural injunction to "pray always" bespeaks this kind of natural inclination. Prayer in this sense is a matter of the very direction of our lives. The Christian is the one who knows that the Father of Jesus is the source of his light, life, and food. Every act and thought somehow represents, however implicitly, his "tendency" toward God. Every real experience of the midst issues in a tendency toward the beyond, a wish for it, a desire to be engulfed in it. The Latin verb "tendere" is translated "to stretch." The experience of human living leads a man of faith and prayer to a kind of inward stretching toward God. Much as leaves stretch to possess the sun, so does a man of the Spirit stretch to possess and be possessed by God.

The great Christian theme of conversion, that is of "turning around," speaks of the moment when a man is willingly seized by God. From then on his direction is toward him and all his actions are the fruit of his willed leaning. Rollo May discovers the human reality of tendency in this sense in psychology: "Each act of consciousness tends toward something and has within it, no matter how latent, some push toward a direction for action."[1] The Christian is one for whom all such tending is toward God, father of Jesus. The Christian stretches.

But there is also a passive sense to the verb "to tend." This sense is caught best in its derivative, "to attend." When we consider tending as careful nurturing, we think of God as waiting us out. But, in speaking in this passive sense, we are the ones

[1]May, *Love and Will*, p. 230.

who do the waiting. To attend is to heed, to listen to, to be present with, to wait for, to be ready for service. An "attendant" is himself submissive. He is the one who must be *patient* in tending, where before we saw nurses tending *patients*. "Attention" is the attitude of readiness. It is an act of courtesy.

This passive sense of tending, attending, brings us to the heart of the Christian understanding of prayer. Prayer, even though it clearly involves active, if tender, participation on the part of men, is an event in which God plays the primary role. Prayer is always a response to the initiative of God. "Prayer," as Balthasar says in the passage referred to above, "is communication, in which God's word has the initiative and we, at first, are simply listeners. What we have to do is, first, listen to God's word and then, through that word, learn how to answer."[2]

This attitude of attentive listening is what Jesus described with the image of servants (*attendants*) awaiting their master's return. Jesus tells his followers to be alert, lamps burning ready, robes gathered clear

[2]von Balthasar, *Prayer*, p. 12.

of the feet so that quick movement is possible. We
have to be ready to move out, to respond at a moment's notice. And the Lord can come "when we least
expect," breaking in on our reveries and disturbing
all our plans. Prayer is being prepared for just such
an unexpected coming. If we are not attentive in
this way, we will miss the moment and the day.

Paul urges attentive listening on us too. He said that
the Spirit of Jesus lives in us, always "crying out
'Abba', 'Father'." To pray is to listen, to tune in, to
pay attention to the prayer of the Spirit within us.
Thus prayer, in this sense, is not so much something
we do as it is a way of seeing and hearing what is
in fact *already* being done. The good news is that we
do not carry the full burden of prayer; the Spirit who
is as much ours as our very own breath prays in us
and for us. Our call is to be courteous and listen, to
heed and pay tender attention. For the prayer the
Spirit prays is of our very own innermost selves.

Up to now we have been exploring some of the
specific meanings of the verb "to tend." Beyond these

the word carries a whole cluster of useful connota-
tions, of which I would like to single out and lift up
three particularly suggestive words; intention, tension,
and intensity.

The word "intention" has long been associated
with praying. We used to speak of praying for a
specific "intention." Actually this word can uncover
yet another small corner of the mystery of prayer for
us if we take a fresh look at it. According to philoso-
pher Edmund Husserl, "Meaning is an *intention* of the
mind."[3] The very way we understand ourselves and
our world rests in some way on what we *intend* our
life to be. If we *intend* our life to be a signal of
transcendence, a relationship with the beyond in our
midst, our life will take on that kind of meaning. To
use an earlier example, if, in turning to the comic-
page puzzle, we *intend* to see the man hidden in the
picnic scene, what we will see will be no mere picnic
scene, but a hiding place for a man, or, with luck,
the man himself. Rollo May puts it this way: "An
intention is a turning of one's attention toward some-

[3]Quoted in Quentin Lauer, *The Triumph of Subjectivity* (New York:
Fordham University Press, 1958), p. 29.

thing. In this sense perception is directed by intentionality."[4] This is why a man of faith and a secular humanist, looking at the same thing or sharing the same experience, can see and experience something different. The man of faith *intends* to meet the man Jesus in the picnic—in life. Prayer—response to the man—flows, therefore, from intention, a choice.

The trouble comes when one tries to see both the "man" and the "picnic scene" with equal clarity. The way human perception seems to work, one must focus on this thing or that, on the man or the picnic, on the tree in the foreground or on the hills in the distance. But as people who take with utter seriousness both the midst and the beyond, both the picnic and the man, we are committed to maintaining the "tension" between what we believe are elements of a single unity. Thus prayer involves us with "tension." To pray is to "stretch" both ways, both toward the neighbor and toward God. We must resist the temptation to let the dichotomizing "tendency" we spoke of earlier infect our "tendency" toward God.

[4]May, *Love and Will*, p. 236.

We are called to be tender with God's presence as it shoots through all our activity and all our being. The stuff of such attention is everything, not just the "holy" moments of sunset or liturgy. Some experiences require more tending than others. The experiences of close human community or of solitude in beautiful natural surroundings or even of death seem more easily to speak to us of the presence of God. This is because, partly at least, these are moments characterized by a quality of experience that we describe with yet another derivative of "tend"; they are moments of "intensity."

The test of faith and of real prayer is tending to God's presence in the experience of the commonplace. One of the happy developments that secularized theology has brought is a new awareness that God is not present only in sacred places or situations. In the past it seemed that we did not have to do much active tending, because God's presence was thought to be available mainly in certain localities (churches, meadows at dawn) and in certain decisions (abstaining from sexual intercourse and from meat). Today, as God has been experienced as receding from nature, morality, and even religion, we can make the discovery that his presence as the totally transcendent is even more total and "intensely" personal than we thought. Now we are hearing the call to nurture our awareness of his total presence everywhere, and not just in the "sacred." If God's presence to us is seen as more intensely personal than we thought, so our presence to him, our tending and tender attention to him, must be more intensely personal than ever.

QUESTIONS FOR DISCUSSION

1. A convert from agnosticism said that she was delighted to find when she became a Catholic that praying, even contemplative prayer, was an art that could be learned and practiced, like gardening or housekeeping. Do you think this is true? Do Catholics generally try to cultivate prayer as an "art" in this sense? If not, why not? Should they?

2. How would you start teaching a child to pray? How were you taught? Do you think children should be made to learn prayers by heart? If so, what kind?

3. Do you think that regular family prayer helps people grow up to be "pray-ers"? Why or why not?

4. What difference is there between praying in a church and praying in an open field? Does being in church help you to pray? Do you pray best in a special position—for example, kneeling? If so, is this just habit or is there some other reason?

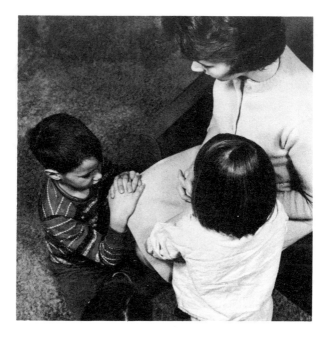

CHAPTER FOUR

faithfulness and spontaneity

Leaves turn spontaneously toward the sun. They wake in the morning with a natural, inner momentum that leads to the finest of movements. To describe prayer as tending toward God is to imply that prayer is an utterly spontaneous reaction of the spirit of man to the approach of God. Prayer arises from an inner tendency of the man of faith, whether it takes the form of spoken word, or symbolic ritual, or silence. This is so despite our common impression that real prayer is an activity for which special training is necessary and which, therefore, is reserved to specialists.

The spontaneity of prayer is in every period a delicate and fragile quality, and it is even more so nowadays. The recent upheavals in theology and liturgical form have called into question our familiar images of God and our old habits of prayer. No longer sure who we are praying to or even if prayer is appropriate, our spontaneity in prayer is interrupted. This sort of interruption, or second thought, about prayer is likely to have its greatest effect on those who are most aware of new thinking in the Church, but it undoubtedly touches everyone who knows at least that changes in God's face are taking place.

These days and this situation bring home to us with unique force the old fact that we are always in *search* of the true God. We are never in possession of him. Thus prayer for us is immediately an act of hope. When prayer is experienced as cultivating, listening, waiting for God's presence, hope takes on a central role. God's presence is not felt continually, indeed it may be felt rarely if ever. To pray is to hope in the face of nonfulfillment. To pray is to wait, lamps burning, for the Lord's coming.

A virtue we speak of less than hope these days is faithfulness. It is less fashionable, but equally crucial. Indeed faithfulness is the flip side of hope. Prayer demands faithfulness now, when little feedback is guaranteed—which is, after all, the only time when faithfulness means very much. We live in a time when the very notion of enduring commitment is regarded in many quarters as naive if not laughable. Value judgments more and more are made on the basis of "feeling like it." Observers comment that our present cultural fear of restrictive commitments form part of a reaction to the immense and inhuman restrictions of a Puritan past. Perhaps so. But reaction alone will not liberate; there is no freedom in hedonism, the flight from faithfulness.

Have we been cultivating hedonism in our prayer? How often have we said to each other, "I pray when I feel like it"? Most of us tend and attend to what we take to be the presence of God at those "boundary moments" of great feeling—moments of pain, beauty, awe. At such times it seems that "God" breaks in on us violently. We feel ourselves lifted, embraced by the beyond. We are "into God." Such experiences

may be described as "action of the Spirit," but I
believe they can be in fact a denial of the all-
present Spirit if they are not rooted in a life of continual attention to God. The New Testament admoni-
tion to "pray always" means tending the presence
of God throughout all life and experience, whether
felt or not, whether "awe-full" or common. Indeed for
those of us for whom the incarnation is the supreme
assurance of God's presence in the world, the magnificent manifestations of the transcendent always remain of secondary importance. The good news of
Christianity is that God is present in the utterly un-
magnificent, in the commonplace. That was the case
with the magnificent Jesus, and it is the case with
and for us. To tend to the presence of God in our
lives is a matter of "re-tending" the places and experiences in which we may have missed him. We tend
and we tend again and again. Not first because we
feel like it, but because we know he is there.

Does all of this mean that spontaneity in prayer

is suspect? Of course not! It cannot be emphasized too much that spontaneity, immediate and unforced, reaches to the true essence of prayer. This is the great truth that those who made a dreary task of prayer, whether old puritans or new priests, lost hold of. This is the great truth that Harvey Cox lifts up when he says that prayer is a "form of play."[1]

But spontaneity is an elusive gift. It has been the experience of most men who have been very good at playing, whether at sports, or music, or prayer, that spontaneity does not come—spontaneously. There is a paradox here, and there is a need to hold onto both halves of a single unity; spontaneity and faithfulness go together. They need each other. We are discovering again the old lesson of art, that without discipline and hard, unrewarding effort there can be no true spontaneity.

If you were a dancer and you joined Martha Graham's ballet troupe, you would work at the exercise bar and in the chorus for ten years before dancing on stage alone. Miss Graham says that it is

[1]Harvey Cox, *The Feast of Fools* (Cambridge, Mass.: Harvard University Press, 1969), p. 147.

only after such a period of discipline and control that a dancer's body is able to be free and truly spontaneous. Of course the expertise required to be one of Martha Graham's dancers is extreme and offers us no final model of the expertise needed to pray. As I said before, prayer is not reserved to experts. All the same, in prayer as in dancing, human spontaneity is as much a matter of perspiration as inspiration. As Bernard Häring says, "The Christian life, it is true, must be spontaneous, a response to the *kairos*, to the God-given opportunity for good here and now. But it would be naive to think that such spontaneity is possible without self-analysis and without conscious purpose."[2]

Unyielding faithfulness to continual practice is as needed for prayer as it is for dancing, or painting, or skiing. Christians received an explicit call from Jesus to absolute, faithful, and continuing commitment to personal prayer; not just to prayer at "great moments." Implicit in the call is the belief that the *kairos*, the right time, is now. Such faithfulness can take the

---

[2]Bernard Häring, "A Modern Approach to the Ascetical Life," in *Worship*, vol. 39, no. 10 (December, 1965), p. 640.

form, for example, of a regular, scheduled commitment to prayer. By building into the rhythm of our
routine lives times of tending the presence of God,
times of listening, times of attention, we do not
guarantee ourselves a felt experience of God, but we
do make it more likely that when God breaks into
the common moments of our life, we will be there
to welcome him.

Häring's phrase "conscious purpose" calls to mind
Rollo May's idea of *intention,* referred to earlier.
When our *attention* to God's presence depends not
primarily on moments of overwhelming feeling now
and then, but on a continuing *intention* to be present
to the presence, the *intensity* of our faith-life will be
greater. May suggests that the intensity of life experiences flows more from the inner intentionality of
a man, which is partly a matter of discipline and de-
cision, than from the events that break in on him.

All of this may seem to make the gift of spontaneous and natural prayer extremely difficult to

attain. In my opinion this is not so. Most mature human beings come to terms in their own ways with the balance between faithfulness and spontaneity in other areas of their lives. When it comes to prayer, achieving this balance is another example of the *tension* involved in all prayer. Unfortunately we are heirs to a tradition in which faithfulness and discipline have been emphasized to the detriment of spontaneity and naturalness. Because of this the belief has been widespread that only certain people—monks, religious, priests, the very pious—are called to a life of prayer. Only they, so it goes, have the time, the energy, the expertise required to pull off prayer successfully. But whether perpetrated by domineering clergy or lazy laymen, to say that the "average Christian," whether bishop or housewife, is not called to a life of prayer is simply untrue. The call to nurture God's presence and await his coming applies equally to all who are "faith-full."

This is not to say that every Christian is called to

a *monastic* style of prayer. Much of the present dis-
illusionment with prayer may in fact be due to the
attempt to make monks of us all. The layman will
attend to the presence of God in ways different from
those used by celibate religious—different, but in
no way less important. Again those members of the
community who accept the call to serve the whole
community by serving the Word, whether as ministers,
catechists, or religious, are called to a life of prayer
like all the baptized. But because they accept a
special responsibility for the Word, the call to faithful
prayer takes on a special seriousness for them. If
they are careless with the presence of God, or if
they ignore it, the whole community suffers in propor-
tion to their responsibility for it. Undoubtedly our
recent poverty of theology, teaching, and preaching
has both contributed to and derived from our common poverty of prayer.

If, indeed, people of our time and place, both the
church-affiliated and the disaffiliated, are searching
for a way to share communion with the extrahuman,

the community of faith, which maintains a tradition of cherishing attention to the presence of God, can make an important contribution to building a human world today. This is why it is important that all Christians heed and accept their call to be "pray-ers," to be tenders of the presence of God. We must be a gathering of people who know well that prayer, far from being the easy pieties of childhood, is the hard thing that happens when a man makes the effort to meet himself and come to terms with God.

QUESTIONS FOR DISCUSSION

1. Should children be made to say morning and night prayers? Using some set form? Do you think it is a good idea for yourself to pray at some set time(s) every day? Using some set forms?
2. Do you think the Sunday Mass obligation is still a good thing? Why or why not?
3. What, if anything, do you think playing and praying have in common? Do you think praying could ever be fun?

4. Do you ever feel like praying? If so, under what circumstances?
5. What would a lay style of prayer be, as different from a monastic one?

CHAPTER FIVE

the tending silence

"The only worthwhile way to talk about prayer is
to say how you pray," said Sebastian Moore.[1] I agree
with him, but I resist him too. It is easier, and a bit
less risky, to deal with what are relatively theoretical
problems. An infinite number of such problems can
be and have been associated with the very idea of
prayer, but finally prayer is not a fit subject for
theorizing. Since prayer is a subject for doing, perhaps it is time for me to say what I do when I pray.
For me prayer is a matter of the tending silence, the
tending solitude, the tending group, and the tending
imagination.

First the tending silence. Silence is more than
the mere absence of noise. Indeed silence can be
quite loud. And though we do not usually think of it
this way, silence can be something we share intimately
with other people. For me prayer seems to be essentially a matter of silence, both solitary silence and

[1]Sebastian Moore and Kevin Maguire, *The Experience of Prayer*
(London: Darton, Longman & Todd, 1969), p. 3.

silence shared. If there is a reason why for me Christ's challenge to "pray always" is, from one point of view, utterly senseless, it is that I am not always silent. Indeed like most people I know, I chatter almost continually, to myself if not to others.

By silence I mean the opposite of chatter. By silence I mean wordlessness. The experience of wordlessness is ambiguous; it can be rich and full of joy, or it can be empty and very hard. Almost always, though, the experience of wordlessness pulls me out of the world I know and control and am comfortable with. Wordlessness seems to break the easy control I exercise over myself and others, since it seems, we use words and noise and chatter as devices of control. In the silence of wordlessness, we meet ourselves and each other as we exist beyond the flesh, beyond dailiness, beyond routine. In silence we come close to ourselves as we truly are and as we are truly called to be. Perhaps this is why, as a people, we take such pains to avoid silence.

We swim in words, our own or some disc

jockey's. The most successful entertainment on radio and television is, as it is fondly known, the "talk" show. We have made an industry of word-producing, not caring that in addition to avoiding wordlessness, we run the risk of destroying words. The word *love* now calls to mind expensive cars, and *sex* calls to mind Ultra-brite. We fight off silence with what has come to be known as "noise pollution." And all because we are shrewd enough to sense that in the experience of wordlessness we might lose ourselves, or, what is often more awe-full, we might find ourselves. This is true because the world of wordlessness is the world of the Spirit. The Spirit not only demands that we let go of ourselves, but he demands that we allow ourselves to be found. The first part of prayer is this: to declare the silence and to tend it wordlessly.

There are, as I experience it, two kinds of wordlessness, and therefore at least two kinds of silence. There is first the hard and sometimes painful wordlessness that happens before the gift of love or union or

vision takes flesh in my life. This wordlessness is a
preparation, a time of cultivation, of hard listening.
It is like the silence of pregnancy. Out of this long
and sometimes nauseous silence, the Word grows
and occasionally is born again. This is the silence the
poet endures as he waits for the muse's gift of the
just-right word that tells him who he is. It is at this
point in prayer, in the wordlessness that precedes
fulfillment, that our earlier notion of faithfulness is
pertinent. Without discipline and a conscious effort
to tend and attend this silence, the Word will be stillborn. Faithful patience in cultivating this preparatory
silence depends·on the conviction that such wordlessness is necessary for the growth of the Word. It
would be easier if the Word of love and union and
fullness always and inevitably grew out of this wordlessness, but it does not. The Word is of the Spirit
and the Spirit blows wherever and whenever he
wants to.

My suggestion that prayer—meeting the Word of
God—depends on a cultivated silence is certainly not

only the product of my own experience. It was out of
the silence of wordlessness that the Word of God
broke in on history. The Christmas liturgy, using lines
from *Wisdom,* puts it this way: "When a profound
stillness compassed everything, your all-powerful
Word, O Lord, bounded from heaven's royal throne."
St. Augustine, grappling with this same truth, wrote,
"In the beginning was the Word. Only wordlessly can
one come to a perception of this."[2] By leaving human
words behind and entering the world of silence, we
enter obscurely and in our own small way the world
where the "beyond" is at home. We enter the "secret
place" Jesus spoke of and discover at once the greatest of silences, the greatest of secrecies, for "The
Word of God," as Balthasar writes, "has come forth
into history from the silence and the secrecy of God."[3]

The hard silence of waiting is what happens most
often when I "decide" to pray. It is the experience of
knowing the Word is not yet here. It feels like this.
I am tired. I stop the useful business that has me
strung a hundred ways. I sit or walk. I kneel. I thumb

[2]Cited in Hans Urs von Balthasar, *Word and Revelation* (New
York: Herder and Herder, 1964), p. 175.
[3]von Balthasar, *Word and Revelation,* p. 189.

the psalms. I begin calculating the business, the busyness again. I stop and come back—come back to this wordless silence that seems so useless. Then enters the old temptation to believe that this silence is futile, is in no way prayer, is indeed silly, unproductive, wasteful. It is all of these and it is at the same time, I believe, the profoundest kind of prayer.

This wordless silence has a place in the liturgy. The communities I share in grapple with it before or after the readings and reflections in the Service of the Word. It is most often the same hard silence, a shared futility. We share the same restlessness to be about the "useful" part of the service. But still we wait in silence, and in this way affirm that we are servants of the Word, attendants, waiters. We are waiters for the Word to take flesh among us. As we are, we are together where Rilke was when he wrote, "I want so much to pray sounds that my hot mouth cannot find."[4]

Occasionally, at great moments of pure gift now and then, the Word does take flesh again. Whether

[4]Rainer Maria Rilke, *Letters to a Young Poet* (New York: Norton, 1954), p. 66.

we are in solitude or community, that fleshing is the ever new and startling experience of the Spirit's breath. It cools our hot mouths. And, as John says, when the Word takes flesh "we behold his glory."

Then it is that we are thrust into the second silence. The beautiful, peace-filled, empty-full experience of being together somehow with who we are and who the mystery-God is. This is the second kind of word-lessness. It is being beyond all words but the great Word of God. Balthasar describes this experience when he writes, "If the Word was silent previously, it is now so rich and luxuriant that further speech and utterance fails."[5] The man of prayer who is also a poet knows that even his best words cannot capture this silence. It is the silence of fullness. To be silent in this way is to allow oneself to be possessed by the present God. It is only in being so possessed by God's presence that we in any way possess it. Ignatius of Antioch wrote that "Whoever really possesses the Word of Jesus can sense also his silence."[6]

This description of the silence of fullness, of union,

[5]Balthasar, *Prayer*, p. 190.
[6]Ignatius of Antioch, *Magister*, 8:2.

of glory, might put you off. We are used to thinking
that this kind of silence is the exclusive property of
contemplatives. But it is everyone's. Recent innova-
tions in religious education have discovered, using
the insights of psychologists such as Piaget, that this
sort of full-silence is common to all of us, especially
when we are children. All men yearn for and are
capable of experiencing in their own ways this
second silence. It is the silence in which we hear, as
Paul says, "The Spirit, who prays in us with un-
speakable groanings."

Though all of us can reach to this wordlessness
in the Word, none of us can manipulate it or manu-
facture it on demand. This silence which joins past
and future is pure gift. For the poet it is the gift given
by the muse. For the man of prayer it is the gift given
by God. It is what makes the hard, empty silence of
daily scheduled attention to God's presence possible.
Though, as it seems to me, the painful silence of
waiting for the Word to "bound down" from its royal
throne is prerequisite to catching hold of the great

silence after the Word has come again, it does not inevitably coax the Word to come. The anguished testimony of great mystics like John or Therese indicates that the great and fulfilling silence can be a rare gift. Yet it is a gift that is promised us, and if we ready ourselves for its coming, we can all dare hope to have it.

The silence of these two kinds of wordlessness is available to us in many ways. The obvious times and places of chosen silence are those of deliberate solitude and within the liturgy in common. Though times of special silence are needed, times of retreat, of aloneness, of liturgy, there is a long Christian tradition that "unspecial" silence should be cultivated too. What we used to describe as a spirit of "recollection" amounted simply to an attitude which seized silence from between the cracks of daily living. Indeed we can even experience silence during speech. The old dichotomy between "mental" and "vocal" prayer has misled us into thinking that silence always

coincides with the absence of sound. The tradition of the litany-prayers, for example, sought to free the spirit from its humdrum by means of a kind of humdrum. The world of inner busyness can be stilled through repetition—whether of saints' names or of "Hail Marys" or of the krishna formula. Psychologists tell us, and I have experienced it, that a release into meditative silence can accompany the habitual repetition of words and actions. There is more wisdom in customs like the rosary, the wheel, and the litanies than present fashion can see.

Beyond these silences associated more or less formally with religion or worship, there are other human experiences of silence which can open us to the Word. One of these is what I call the "silence of alienation." This is the frustrating experience of wordlessness at times when a word is very much needed. It is what happens when, in the midst of true communion, two friends are startled by a stare that slips between them. It is what happens, when, having been offered the true word of love, I find no response coming out of myself. This silence is a moment when we confront the utter "beyondness" of each other and we are afraid.

This silence can be the occasion of true prayer for it is a moment of utter yearning for the one, fully faithful and always open Word of love. This silence calls up from us petition, sorrow, hope. This silence calls from God his enabling and healing Word. It is the silence of chaos that calls out for creation.

QUESTIONS FOR DISCUSSION

1. Is silence necessary for prayer? Is prayer possible, for instance, on a bus or at a ball game?
2. Do you think there is enough silence in the present Mass? How and when might more and better silence be introduced?
3. How would you go about teaching a child to pray in silence, in the sense explained in this chapter? Were you taught to pray that way? Do people need teaching?

4. Do you think that a kind of silence can come when you are repeating a prayer-formula, as in the rosary? Did you ever pray the rosary? Do you now? Why or why not?

CHAPTER SIX

the tending solitude,
the tending group

Albert Camus, in his short story "The Artist At Work,"[1] relates the experience of a successful artist who struggles for a long time over what his disciples expect to be a major new direction in painting. Throughout his struggle the artist works alone in his loft. When finally he emerges from it, his followers rush in to see the finished canvas. It is large and still white. The only brush strokes are fine and concentrated in the very center. Everyone is amazed to see that the strokes form a word, but no one can agree on what the word is. It is either "solidary" or "solitary." No one knows which it is for sure. Camus ends his story on the question.

The solidary and the solitary in human life are so closely related that it is easy to mix them up. They are so intermingled that, so it seems to me, unless one

[1] In *Exile and the Kingdom* (New York: Vintage Books, 1965).

understands both, he can understand neither. Earlier we saw that one of the most destructive dichotomies of true prayer has been the hard division between the "private" and the "common." Indeed we have forced ourselves to feel at times as if we had to choose between the two. So it is that we have recently put such emphasis on communal prayer that it forms the exclusive prayer-experience for many of us.

My understanding of prayer as involving *tension* as well as *attention* comes into play here. Real prayer requires the real experience both of the solitary and the solidary, because the solitary and the solidary imply and require each other. Prayer in aloneness leads to and comes from prayer in fellowship—and the opposite is also true.

Solitude is essential. There are times when both silence and the Word should be tended to alone. If there is true continuity between community and solitude, we can care for each other together only by going apart at times. I go apart often. I have given up trying to guarantee that my yearnings after solitude are always wholesome, that is, always the sort of pinings that prepare me to enter again and more fully into fellowship. Undoubtedly some of my going apart represents a selfish or fearful refusal of others. Escape can disguise itself masterfully as retreat, and it is hard to know on a given day which is what. But even so, retreat is essential and a rhythm of going away to be alone and coming back to be together is a rhythm that is denied only at high cost to humanness and to tendency toward God.

My solitude is a quest both for the Word and for the silence. I search out the Word mainly in the scriptures, but in other ways too. I am a writer and I search out the Word by writing. For me the struggle with words, small *w*, is the same as the struggle with the Word, large *W*. Most often this quest is a matter of pencil poised and not writing. It is attention. It is the first kind of wordlessness. Many empty hours seem to mark the usual pattern. But occasionally the gift happens, and the Word enfleshes itself in me. I find at times small words to write and one large Word to meet. And I behold glory—whether critics do or not. Solitude in this way tends me, while I tend and attend the Word.

There is a way in which the most important things we have to do, we have to do alone. There is a way in which we have to meet ourselves and we have to meet God in utter aloneness. There are times when we cannot deny the fact that however rich the gift of love might be in our lives, we are alone. Rilke put it this way; "To speak of solitude again, it becomes always clearer that this is at bottom not something that one can take or leave. We are solitary."[2] I am speaking of the aloneness of the mature and human person, not of the sociopath or narcissist, even though mature aloneness will probably always have a margin of immaturity about it. I am speaking of the aloneness of courage, even though it will probably always have a margin of fear about it.

The person who allows himself to experience his aloneness discovers an unparalleled insecurity which, paradoxically, invites abandonment to something in-

[2]Rilke, *Letters to a Young Poet*, p. 66.

expressibly greater. There is a nakedness about being alone in this way. All the familiar markings and trappings on which our eyes customarily rest are gone. It is like being lifted to the top of a great mountain range. The most horrid fear of falling coexists with the exhilaration of a new world opened out to us. For a man of faith, the experience of being alone is an experience of choosing the totally other— God—who reaches out from an aloneness of his own. For Christians the point of the experience of aloneness is not the *feeling* we get or the achieving of some kind of solitary "high." There can be a pseudo-mysticism about monkishness. For us the point of aloneness is the person we meet there and to whose call we reply. The person of God.

Those of us who are Christians can learn from Jesus what it is to be alone. He was a man who cherished his solitude, who went apart often. Yet often his solitude seemed to be a continuing struggle, a Jacob-like wrestling with God. The only moments of Jesus' life in which the gospels show him hesitant and

insecure are moments of his aloneness. The desert
was a terrifying place for the nomad people, and as
one of them, it was so for Jesus. Yet of the desert
Jesus made a second home.

Jesus, who shows us what it is to be alone, shows
us what it is to be together, too. Even at the hour of
his most intense solitude, in the garden on the night
before he died, Jesus made sure his close friends
were nearby. Though apparently he did not share
his struggle with them fully, for they were "at a distance," and though he seemed to know that night
was a night of aloneness, still Jesus wanted and
needed his friends to be there, "watching," "attending," "praying." His pain at their tired and repeated
failure to be with him then says much about the importance for each of us of the tending group.

Solitude, silence, and the Word exist for the
sake of communion. Communion with God, certainly,
but communion with God implies communion with
other men. And so it is that prayer is a matter of the
tending group. We must pray together, we must

"watch" with each other. If we do not, we are tending the presence of anything but God. We need to embody and make visible our faith that in meeting God we meet each other. This is for me the meaning of the Catholic Church's unromantic and somewhat law-obsessed discipline about regular Mass *attendance*, and of its continuing, if recently obscured, insistence on the sacraments as communal acts of worship.

Of course the Eucharist is the group's chief time of tendency toward the presence of the Father of Jesus, much as the meal serves most human beings, in spite of T.V. dinners, as the chief time of tending to one another. The liturgy, even in this confused time of change, makes it possible for people together to experience both the tending Word and the tending silence. Group prayer awakens us again to the fact that this universe has its meaning and value precisely because there are others who "watch" with us, others who are not merely *there* but *here*. Faith is a gift that does not come to us in isolation. God's intrusion into our lives is mediated. It happens in and through and with all the intrusions into our isolation that are our relationships with other persons. Our openness to the good news of the Father's love for us is intertwined with our openness to the good news of our friend's love for us. Our need as friends and as people to respond to God with and through each other derives from the fact that God's approach comes to us with and through each other.

Liturgy shared is language; and it is language finally, not silence, that makes man fully human. Fully human language carries its own silence. The symbol used by the author of the Acts of the Apostles to describe the unity of the first Christians and the effect on them of the Spirit was language. The friends of Jesus, having experienced the fiery approach of the Spirit on Pentecost, discovered and expressed their fellowship, their peoplehood, by speaking in a language that gathered all languages—those of Parthians as well as Medes—into one tongue of magnificent communion.

We have our being and meaning in different groups of differing importance. For the Christian the prime group for tending God's presence is the group which shares one faith, one Lord, one baptism—the Church. Within the Christian Church there are traditions from which each of us derive an identity and a self-understanding and with whom we ordinarily worship. Beyond that it is my experience that those groups in which we find ourselves most attentive to each other and to our true selves are the groups which call out for common attention to the Word of God. For most this is probably a matter of the intimate group, the family, the friend-group, neighbors and colleagues, and, ideally, the community group, the parish. Though the quality of liturgy available to such groups at present varies, the reform of liturgical practice makes a variety of group worship experiences possible. In addition to formal liturgy, all groups in which we find human support and meaning should wherever possible pursue less formal and more adventurous forms of common attention to God's presence.

My tending groups right now are two. I live with a group of Paulist brothers. Some of us share attention to the presence of God each morning for a time of scripture and silence. I live also with students at a large university. Some of us share attention to God each day with the Word and the Bread. We gather in the shared conviction that when two or more of us are together, there is always a third. We do not gather chiefly out of hopes to "experience community," though community is essential. We do not gather for the delight primarily of human "sensitivity," though sensitivity is required. We gather to concentrate on, to celebrate, and to share the ever-third person who comes in the mystery of Word and silence. This third is, we believe, Jesus—the focus for us of God.

QUESTIONS FOR DISCUSSION

1. Should children be taught to pray by themselves or is family prayer enough? Should children be

obliged to attend family prayers? What kind of prayers, if any, would you like in your family?

2. Do you think that wanting to be "alone with God" can be an escape from involvement in the lives of other human beings? What do you think of the lives of contemplative religious, like the Carmelite nuns or the Trappists? What do you think of hermits? Have you ever wanted to be one?

3. Many of the changes in the mass were meant to help people take part in it as a community rather than a collection of solitary worshipers. Do you think they have been successful in this? What might help?

4. Can a large congregation become a "tending group"? If so, how?

CHAPTER SEVEN

the tending imagination

"If ever I get into heaven," said the great theologian Karl Barth, "I must confess that I shall first ask for Mozart, and only then for Augustine and Thomas, Luther, Calvin and Schleiermacher." Me too, though I must confess that I would ask for Miles Davis before I would ask for Mozart. It is significant that a theologian like Barth ranks as his cherished man someone from the arts rather than his own field. He wants to be greeted at the gate of heaven by someone from the world of music, the world of imagination. I am not surprised, for what we call the imagination is as close to a man's heart (even a theologian's) as his blood.

Prayer, as we have seen, is a matter of hope, spontaneity, faithfulness, silence, Word, solitude, and group. All of these elements meet for me in the central human faculty, the imagination. Prayer is a matter of the tending imagination. Because we have the power to imagine, we have the power to engage the realities of life. The function of the imagination is to bring together in a cohesive and available union all the million impulses and contradictions we experience. Earlier I argued that one of the chief obstacles to prayer is the discontinuity we create between the poles of natural human unities. Imagination is the reverse of the dichotomizing tendency in man. Samuel Coleridge, who formulated the great modern definition of imagination, described it as the "reconciler of opposites." Our thinking and feeling, our wanting and doing, our living and dying, do not break us apart finally because we can make *images* of their deep unity. As William Lynch suggests, the capacity to hope coincides with the capacity to *imagine* a resolution of our contradictions.[1]

When I said earlier that tending the presence of God implies "tension," I was hinting at the role of imagination in prayer. The imagination is our stretching faculty. In the last chapter, I lifted up the gospel *image* of Jesus at Gethsemane to show the interrelat-

[1]William F. Lynch, *Images of Hope* (Baltimore: Helicon, 1965).

edness of his needs for the solitary and the solidary. In a larger way, Jesus serves as *the* great image of the interrelatedness of God and man. Karl Barth's wry preference of the world of imagination over the world of intellectual theology derives from the fact, finally, that the good news is addressed not just to the human mind, nor just to human feeling, but to the whole man. The good news is addressed to the imagination.

To be attentive to the presence of God is to *imagine* that God is indeed present. The good news that God is in fact present to us as a loving Father comes to us in images. An image is any concrete event or picture which focuses both the insight of thought and the power of feeling. We know what we know of Jesus primarily through the imaginative statements made about him in the scriptures. Jesus himself used an imaginative kind of folk-talk because he was talking to folks. Folks imagine. The imagination, appealing as it does to sights and smells and memories and mind and anger and warmth, engages the whole man.

It is the whole man who prays. Real prayer is imaginative. The tradition of Christian prayer tells us this. The prayer-language of the Church is metaphorical, made of images. We live in a time when many of the traditional metaphors—heaven, God as Father, the Sacred Heart, and so on—are suspect. That is as it should be, for different ages live with different metaphors. Living as we do between two ages, it should not be surprising that the tried and true religious metaphors, symbols, and images are up for grabs.

Some observers warn, however, that the very idea of metaphor is threatened during the Catholic transition now occurring. They suggest that those of us who are Catholics are in danger of losing the rich imaginative sense our tradition has maintained, just at the time the Reformed Churches are discovering it. In some places Protestants are putting on vestments as quickly as Catholics are taking them off.

The conviction that the whole man prays has been nourished by customs now under scrutiny. There has been an unarticulated "ecology of prayer," with concern for the total environment of praying-man being manifested by "sacredness" in space, in gesture, in clothing, in sound, in smell. The senses must be so engaged in an activity if it is the activity of the whole man. Though it will undoubtedly change in form and style, a commitment to imaginative and "sensible" prayer will continue as an ecology of prayer.

Prayer issues from the same place in man in which poetry is born. We will as a people rediscover the full sense of prayer when as a people we rediscover the sense of poetry. Poetry exists as an imaginative articulation of man's consciousness (sensibility, feeling, thought) at his most alive and aware. Man praying, I believe, is man most alive and aware. And so prayer leads naturally into poetry.

The problem with prayer in our days is not with the metaphors we find so bothersome. The problem is with us. If we cannot pray with rich human images, it is because we do not live with rich human images. When it comes to imagination we share in a widespread cultural poverty. The present unsatisfactory state of education, of theater, pop music, government, and, I would add, prayer, is, according to Benjamin De Mott, "traceable largely to obliviousness, habitual refusal to harry private imaginations into constructing the innerness of other lives."[2]

If I urge that we tend more carefully to our imaginative powers in prayer, it is not simply for the sake of aesthetic experience that I do so. It is for the sake of our tendency toward God. Kafka held that "All art is a form of prayer," but I would say that there is an essential distinction between the intent of any work of art and prayer. It is this: every work of art, whether music or poetry or ballet, concentrates on *what* is conveyed to and through the imagination. Prayer, on the other hand, concentrates on a *who;* prayer concentrates on the person who conveys the message; prayer concentrates on God. Thus, art and

---

[2]Benjamin De Mott, *Supergrow: Essays and Reports on Imagination in America* (New York: Dutton, 1969), p. 117.

prayer are not the same thing, though both engage the imagination and though they can on occasion coincide.

Art and prayer do, however, have more in common than we ordinarily think. I am not urging imagination in prayer simply as a technique or "way to pray effectively." I am suggesting that it is impossible to pray without in some way engaging the imagination, for God's presence is available to us only imaginatively. When the poet who wrote the Book of Genesis said that "in his own *image* God created man," he was saying that the most concrete and immediate presence of God would be man. God *imagined* man. An image points to, stands for, and participates in the reality of what is imaged. The "midst," to use Bonhoeffer's terminology again, points to, stands for, and participates in the reality of the "beyond."

When the author of John's gospel chooses the notion of the *Word* as the central idea of the incarnation, he is implying that the Son of God is related to the Father as the imaginative expression of who the Father is. God has chosen to speak to us in and through images. The scriptures serve as the touchstone of revelation, and therefore prayer, because they gather the primordial images chosen by God to unhide himself; the images of Israel, of covenant, of judge, of father, of faithful husband, of deliverer, of punisher, of Word, of baby, of suffering servant, of crucified, of risen one, of breath, of people.

When in prayer we seek to reply to God, we reply in and through images. One of the ways we do this is through what has commonly been called the "prayer of petition." Through the prayer of request, we express, by means of a concrete and focused *image,* that we realize that all of human life is a gift of God. Our specific need or concern, the issue that brings us to our knees, becomes in this way an *image* of our response to God. To ask God for some good thing is to affirm through the image of that good thing that we depend on him and hope in him.

The world of imagination is not the world of magic, just as prayers of petition, properly understood, are not magical in their intent. J. R. R. Tolkien, in discussing the imaginative world of fairy tales, makes a useful distinction here.[3] Through imagination we are able to create and be in what Tolkien calls a "secondary world." We live our daily lives in the "primary world." The secondary world is not opposed to the primary in some platonic sense, but participates in the reality of the primary world. The secondary world is the realm of mystery. It is what we experience in silence. It is not a problem-free realm to which troubled men can flee, as prayer is no flight from reality. The secondary world is our own daily world, good and bad, fun and hard, but it is experienced in depth and opens out into mystery.

The world of imagination is not a magical world, though like prayer it seems to have the qualities of magic if examined carelessly. According to Tolkien the world of imagination is characterized by enchantment, not magic. "Enchantment," he says, "produces a secondary world into which both the designer and the spectator can enter."[4] They meet each

[3] J. R. R. Tolkien, *The Tolkien Reader* (New York: Ballantine Books, 1966), p. 52.
[4] *Ibid.*, p. 52.

other and are satisfied to share the mystery of the place. When we pray we encounter God, the designer, in mystery. We do not attempt to manipulate or control him. We are filled with fascination and awe for him. Magic, on the other hand, is manipulative. It intends to drag God out of the world of mystery, out of the secondary world into the primary, and make use of him there. As Tolkien says, "Magic produces or pretends to produce an alteration in the primary world."[5]

Man's powers of fantasy, imagination, and prayer aspire to enchantment, not to magic. In the words of an earlier section, enchantment is "tender," while magic is harsh. Whenever we enter the world of mystery, and it is in this world that we pray, the temptation to confuse enchantment and magic plagues us. The common association of magical intent and prayer of request attests to this. Our petitions to God function not as a demand on him to break into our world and, say, make the Americans and Vietnamese drop

[5]*Ibid.*, p. 53.

their guns. They function rather as images of our attitude toward him and toward our world.

We know that God leaves nature to its own course and history to man's own course. We know, in other words, that God will not break into the primary world and change it because we ask him to. But we also know that nature's own course and man's own course are not removed from God's own course, but are in some way intermingled with it. We know that, according to the promise of the resurrection, the primary world and the secondary world, the world of dailiness and the world of mystery, will meet at the end. Indeed these worlds have already met in Jesus Christ, and because of that, we know that God does take totally surprising initiatives for the good of man. Our prayer for peace is mainly a prayer that we will be able to do what we must do to get the guns dropped. But beyond that, because prayer thrusts us into the mystery of God, it is a reminder that God surprises us continually. Prayer is a hope that we will be surprised again soon.

QUESTIONS FOR DISCUSSION

1. What images does the word, "God," immediately bring to mind?

2. What kind of images are used in the Our Father, the Hail Mary, the Creed? Read one of the psalms and discuss the images it uses. Which are most helpful?

3. Do you think that most statues and "holy pictures" are helpful or harmful in giving us images to think about God, Christ, His Mother, the saints? What kind do you find helpful, if any?

4. If you carry a St. Christopher medal or holy statue in your car, is this necessarily using religion as magic? How about praying to St. Anthony when you lose something?

5. Do you think that praying for some favor will induce God to grant it? If not, what is the point of any "prayers of petition"?

CHAPTER EIGHT

the practice of prayer today

What is prayer from where we are? What will the practice of prayer today look like? In these last few pages I will try to pull together the bits and pieces of ideas and inclinations that have sprinkled themselves through the preceding chapters.

We began by taking a look at some of the ways in which prayer has become less a matter of relating to a person than of solving a problem. For those of us with a personal investment in the past, the problem with prayer is part of our problem with our old ideas of the Church and of God. How do you pray when someone keeps telling you that God does not want your prayers, but only your work toward the welfare of others? Or, even more perplexing, how do you pray when someone keeps telling you that post-industrial man is post-theistic, too? For those of us who are younger, the problem of prayer is related to the problem of our whole youth culture. How do you pray without falling into the traps of pseudomysticism in which the "experience" takes on more importance than the "other," whose presence prayer tends?

In these pages I have talked little *about* God. I have talked a great deal about some of the experiences that seem to go with talking to him. My assumption has been that, while we can never fully express God or talk with complete accuracy about him, we can talk to him, and we can be present to his presence. I have assumed without embarrassment that God is a "person" who "cares" enough to send the very best—himself. I believe that the practice of prayer begins with this conviction. It ends with it, too, for after all our talk about the "experience" of prayer, what is important is the conviction that prayer is not something we do only for ourselves. We do it for God, not because he needs our attention, but because he wants it.

There is much confusion about prayer today, and much neglect of the practice of it, not only because of the confusion about God and the turmoil in the churches, but because of some more fundamental human problems that plague us. Chief of these has been our tendency to dichotomize, to separate and break apart elements of what are in fact unities. We have done this often with the hope of strengthening our commitment to one or other of the polarized elements, yet in the end, we find ourselves less committed than before. Thus, we neglect prayer in the name of service, and before long, find ourselves asking about the very meaning of our service. We neglect discipline and faithfulness in prayer in the name of spontaneity, and find ourselves, before long, with no prayer at all in our lives. We neglect silence for the sake of communication and find ourselves with no communion. We neglect solitude for the sake of community and find ourselves wondering why there is nothing to say. We neglect imagination with its color and movement and festivity for the sake of simplicity and functionalism and find that prayer is boring.

The practice of prayer today must be a matter

of *tension,* of stretching both ways, of keeping hold of both sides of each unity. Prayer will be tender of both the midst and the beyond, of both the solidary and the solitary. This kind of prayer will be hard-nosed, more a matter of courage than of piety. Prayer will be for us what it was for the whole line of battered men, Jacob and Job and Moses and Jeremiah and Jesus, who, when prayer called them out of comfort into struggle with the living God, prayed more.

But prayer will be tender too. Prayer will be sensitive to God's presence because that presence is elusive and fragile and easily missed. The man who prays keeps hearing over and over the words of John the Baptist, "In your midst there stands one you don't know." The man who prays will continually discover that he has wandered off, that he has fallen asleep on the watch, that there were faint hints of God intended for him only and they were missed. The man who prays will hear over and over the words of Jesus to Philip, "I've been with you so long and you don't know me yet!" The man who prays will know that his prayer is only a groping toward the God who is never caught and held.

Because the true God is always beyond our possession, there is a way in which true prayer is always just beyond our grasp too. In trying to uncover the practice of prayer today, we should remember that as long as our ideas of God remain obscure and as long as our knowledge of ourselves remains partial, there will be an obscurity and a partiality about our praying. I take it that something of this is inevitable. It is probable that there will always be a margin of superstition about our prayer, just as there will always be a margin of unbelief about our belief.

If it is so that our praying is mixed in this way, it seems to me that we should have a twofold response to this condition. On the one hand, we should be ever alert to possibilities of growth, and to purging our prayer of all superstition and unbelief. On the other hand, we should begin from where we are. Some recent commentators make it sound as if the only one capable of authentic prayer is God himself, and not all of them seem to be sure that he is. Every human person, even the most superstition-ridden, is called to and capable of prayer. If we are unsure of our ability, or if questions of faith lead us to hesitate at a time when we would tend God's presence, that is all the more reason not only why we should pray, but why we should feel as if we can. The man who never wonders about the very possibility of prayer and talks as if it is a simple matter of tuning in Telstar, either possesses gifts Jesus himself was deprived of or has deceived himself cruelly. Part of the knowledge of prayer is knowing what the felt absence of prayer is like.

It is to say nothing of prayer to say that "prayer is life." Yet the practice of prayer must spring from the full context of life as we live it. The God whose presence we tend in prayer must be the same God we meet and serve constantly, even if not explicitly. He is the God whose face we discover in the scriptures and especially in the image of the man Jesus. The

moments of explicit attention to God must spring from all the moments when, though not praying, we are implicitly attentive to his presence. Anything, therefore, can become the content of prayer; joy at success on the job can become joyful thanksgiving, and anger at the injustice of life for others can become anger at God. Anything which is the content of our life can become the content of our conscious life with God.

To be attentive to God's presence today means being open and attentive to new forms of prayer. Some twelfth-century monk's idea of praying was never intended to exhaust the human spirit's ways of listening to God. Nor could it, in any case. At a time like ours, when a new burst of creativity and innovation has swept over our whole world, it would be surprising if men of faith did not devise new ways of being sensitive to the beyond in our midst. In some ways this kind of innovation is beginning to occur in the liturgical forms of Christian prayer. Expressions of the contemporary imagination are beginning to influence community prayer through music and poetry and dance and forms of visual media. The challenge now is to be as creative and imaginative in devising forms of prayer for our time as Renaissance men of faith were in devising forms for theirs.

If we should not be afraid of new forms of prayer, neither should we fear old ones. There is more wisdom in the prayer traditions to which we are heirs than is fashionable to admit. There is, I believe, positive, indeed irreplaceable, value in the tradition of regular rhythm in our praying. The custom of following monastic hours may not be suited to our lives, but the custom of some daily attention to God's Word, especially in the scriptures, is as valid as ever. A regular commitment to times of tending silence seems to me to be necessary as well if faith is to be nurtured into life.

The fact that we all too easily forget is that being human has something extrahuman about it. For all that the sciences of life and man can show us, they leave us, finally, short of discovering who we are. For we never know fully who we are, indeed we never *are* fully who we are until we stand with some consciousness before God. The gathering of people who are the Church exists to proclaim this to each other and to the world: that there is about being man a Being—God—who is not an indifferent observer nor an enemy but a friend. Indeed he is a father, the father of Jesus. This proclamation, this mission believers share, is a matter mainly of the way we live with each other and the world. But it is also and especially a matter of the way we live with God. It is a matter of constant, faithful and evermore authentic prayer.

Each of us is different, and many of us serve different functions and live different styles of life within the community of faith. What the practice of prayer means for each of us within these larger differences will vary too. Prayer for the family, prayer for the celibate, prayer for the ordained, prayer for the student—it may all look different, but it will be, finally, the same thing. It will be tending the presence of God. It will involve faithfulness and hope and spontaneity and silence and the Word and solitude and community and imagination. In the end it will all be the prayer of the Spirit who lives in us, praying unspeakably, "Father!"

If after all this, you are saying to yourself, "Yes, but you have not told me *how* to pray," you are right on. If you are wondering what prayer ultimately means, or whether to abandon it and move on, I have not yet, nor can I, come to tell you why you should not. I have only, indeed *could* only, have shared some of what prayer means to me and some of why I have not abandoned it.

As for you the only decisive answer to your question is waiting to be discovered within your own secret place. If you are wondering how to pray, all anyone can say, finally, is, "Just pray!" After all these words, there is no other way of discovering what prayer is and why it is precious than through praying. If you wanted to know what poetry is about, I would talk some about what it is to me, and then I would suggest that you write a poem. And I would promise you that great discoveries are waiting to be made, that great words are waiting to be spoken, and that the great mystery of man is waiting to be met.

Prayer and poetry. Poetry perhaps, but certainly prayer, for prayer means intensely greater discoveries waiting, the one only Word waiting, and the great mystery-God waiting for you.

QUESTIONS FOR DISCUSSION

1. Do you think God needs your prayer? Do you think he wants it? Why?
2. Is your praying characterized more by "comfort" or by "tension." Does it include elements of both?
3. Do you think there is a margin of superstition about your prayer? If so, what is your attitude toward it?
4. Have you ever lit a candle in church? If so, what did it mean to you? If not, what do you think of the custom?
5. Could an intense feeling of anger be the content

of prayer for you? How? Could you imagine yourself shaking your fist at God?

6. Has going through this booklet and discussing it
helped solve any of your problems about praying?
Has it made you want to try to pray more?

SUGGESTIONS FOR FURTHER READING

Berger, Peter. *A Rumor of Angels*. New York: Doubleday, 1969.

von Balthasar, Hans Urs. *Prayer*. New York: Sheed & Ward, 1961.

Cox, Harvey. *Feast of Fools*. Cambridge, Mass.: Harvard University Press, 1969.

Haughton, Rosemary. *Transformation of Man*. New York: Paulist Press, 1967.

May, Rollo. *Love and Will*. New York: Norton, 1969.

Moore, Sebastian, and Maguire, Kevin. *Experience of Prayer*. London: Darton, Longman & Todd, 1969.

Novak, Michael. *Theology of Radical Politics*. New York: Herder and Herder, 1969.

Picard, Max. *World of Silence*. Chicago: Regnery, 1961.

Rahner, Hugo. *Man at Play*. New York: Herder and Herder, 1965.

Rahner, Karl. *On Prayer*. New York:Paulist Press, 1968.

Raines, Robert. *Creative Brooding*. New York: Macmillan, 1968.

Ryan, Mary Perkins. *Psalms '70: A New Approach to Old Prayers*. Dayton, Ohio: Pflaum, 1969.